THE
healthy heart
COOKBOOK

DAWN STOCK

p

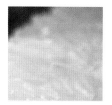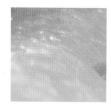

This is a Parragon Publishing Book
This edition published in 2005

Parragon Publishing
Queen Street House
4 Queen Street
Bath
BA1 1HE
UK

Designed and produced by
THE BRIDGEWATER BOOK COMPANY

Introduction, Nutritional Facts and Analyses: *Charlotte Watts*
Photography: *Clive Bozzard-Hill*
Home economist: *Philippa Vanstone*
Stylist: *Angela Macfarlane*

The publishers would like to thank the following companies for the loan
of props: *Dartington Crystal, Marlux Mills, Maxwell & Williams, Lifestyle Collections, Viners & Oneida, Typhoon, and John Lewis.*

Printed in China

ISBN: 1-40543-687-5

NOTES FOR THE READER

This book uses imperial, metric, or US cup measurements. Follow the same units of measurement throughout; do not mix imperial and metric. All spoon measurements are level, unless otherwise stated: teaspoons are assumed to be 5 ml and tablespoons are assumed to be 15 ml.

Individual vegetables such as potatoes are medium. Salt is not included in the recipes and should only be added to foods at the table where absolutely necessary. Milk used in the recipes is skim or semiskim to help limit the fat content of the meal. The recipes have been made with a reduced-fat and -sugar content in accordance with healthy eating guidelines. However, this means that they will not keep fresh for as long a period of time as their higher-fat and -sugar alternatives. This is particularly the case with cakes, so storage advice has been included where appropriate.

Some of the recipes require stock. If you use commercially made bouillon granules or cubes, these can have a relatively high salt content, so do not add any further salt. If you make your own stock, keep the fat and salt content to a minimum. Don't sauté the vegetables before simmering—just simmer the vegetables, herbs, and meat, poultry, or fish in water and strain. Meat and poultry stocks should be strained, cooled, and refrigerated before use so that the fat from the meat rises to the top and solidifies—it can then be easily removed and this reduces the saturated fat content of the meal. Homemade stocks should be stored in the refrigerator and used within two days, or frozen in usable portions and labeled.

The values of the nutritional analysis for each recipe refer to a single serving, or a single slice where relevant. They do not include the serving suggestion. Where a range of portions is given the nutritional analysis figure refers to the mid-range figure. The calorific value given is in KCal (Kilocalories). The carbohydrate figure includes starches and sugars, with the sugar value then given separately. The fat figure is likewise the total fat, with the saturated part then given separately.

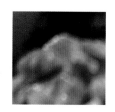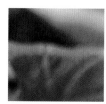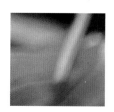

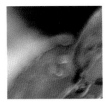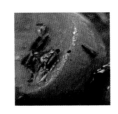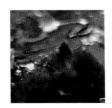

contents

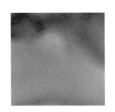

Introduction

We spend a lot of time and money looking after our outward appearance and increasingly feel the need to halt the signs of aging, for instance, by concealing our gray hairs or applying antiwrinkle creams to our skins. However, we often don't pay nearly the same amount of attention to the condition of our internal organs—the heart in particular. Given its fundamental importance to our entire wellbeing, we really should take time to think about our heart's state of health and its day-to-day maintenance.

Diet and Exercise Caution

Before embarking on any diet, you should consult your doctor, especially if you have recently been ill or have special dietary or medical requirements, or if you are pregnant or breastfeeding, are a child, or are elderly.

Before taking up any exercise program, you should consult your doctor, especially if you are worried about any aspect of your health, particularly if you suffer from respiratory problems such as asthma or bronchitis, or suffer from heart disease, high blood pressure, back trouble, joint pains, or arthritis, or if you have recently had an operation or been ill.

The trend in the US is for an increasing number of people to be overweight. We are eating a diet that is increasingly higher in fat, sugars, and salts and engaging in less exercise. If we add stress, smoking, and excessive drinking to this lifestyle, we are undoubtedly putting extra strain on our bodies and our hearts.

But it's never too late to start looking after yourself. The recipes in this cookbook show you how to adopt a healthy eating lifestyle, by reducing the saturated fat, sugar, and salt and increasing the fruit, vegetables, and fiber in your diet, in simple and appetizing ways. Even if you only pick up a few of the practical dietary messages in this cookbook, you will enjoy the benefits—including the pleasure of eating great food!

We all have good days and bad days. If you have a meal out to celebrate a special occasion that is high in calories and full of fat, don't give up in despair—just be more careful about what you eat for the next few days. And remember that your healthy eating meals should outnumber the excessive, indulgent ones.

Hard Heart Facts

Coronary heart disease is a major cause of death and illness in the US and accounts for over 700,000 deaths per year. Over 10 percent of adults in the US have some form of heart disease. Women should not be complacent—there are concerns that they may be placing themselves at a greater risk as increasing numbers of younger women are eating unhealthily, drinking more alcohol, smoking, and exercising less.

Some factors that increase our risk of heart disease cannot be influenced, for example, if there is a family history of heart disease or if you have diabetes. Another contributory factor over which we have no control is aging. However, we can all help reduce our risk of heart disease by eating a healthy diet, exercising more, and stopping smoking.

Reduce Your Risk

You can reduce your risk of coronary heart disease by:

- Not being overweight.
- Eating less saturated fat.
- Eating five portions of fruit and vegetables a day.
- Eating fewer salty snacks and by not adding salt to your food.
- Eating fewer sugary snacks and drinks.
- Drinking moderate amounts of alcohol and not exceeding the recommended guidelines regularly.
- Not smoking.
- Exercising regularly—three hours of cardiovascular exercise per week is recommended.
- Reducing your stress levels and learning to relax.
- Eating a healthy diet, which can help to balance and reduce harmful cholesterol levels.

Eating a balanced, healthy diet may help reduce your risk of coronary heart disease and benefit you by:

- Helping you to reach or maintain a healthy body weight and so reduce the strain on your heart.
- Helping you to lower your blood cholesterol level.
- Keeping your blood pressure down.
- Helping to prevent the unwanted fatty layer from building up in the inside walls of your arteries, which, over time, can restrict blood flow.
- Helping to prevent blood clots called thrombosis forming. Thrombosis can ultimately cause heart attacks and strokes.
- Increasing your chances of survival if you do suffer a heart attack.

Eat Your Way to a Healthy Heart

By following these simple guidelines, you will improve your diet and help to look after your heart.

Reduce Excess Weight

There is no question that being overweight puts a strain on your entire body since it has to work harder to carry you about, putting a strain on your joints, organs, and especially your heart. Being overweight can also increase your risk of high blood pressure and can unbalance the ratio of good to bad cholesterol in the blood and therefore increase your risk of coronary heart disease. Reducing the fat in your diet is a good starting point to losing excess weight, but remember to consult a doctor before starting any diet program. If you don't need to lose weight but you plan to reduce the amount of fat in your diet, you will need to replace these lost calories by eating more starchy foods—see page 8 for advice.

Eat Fewer Saturated and Trans Fats

Although a small amount of fat is needed in our diet to provide essential vitamins and fatty acids that our bodies cannot alone provide, most people need to reduce the amount of saturated fat that they eat. It is important to understand about the different fats we eat in our foods, so that we can make healthier food choices. There are two types of fat in the diet: saturated and unsaturated. The unsaturated fats include polyunsaturated and monounsaturated fats.

Saturated fats are the fats we should be eating less of because they raise blood cholesterol levels more than anything else in the diet, which in turn encourages the development of fatty deposits in the walls of the arteries and can cause the blood to thicken and clot. Narrowing arteries and clots (also called thrombus) can, over time, restrict the flow of blood and result in a heart attack or stroke. Saturated fats are found mainly in dairy products such as butter, cheese, yogurt, cream, milk, and

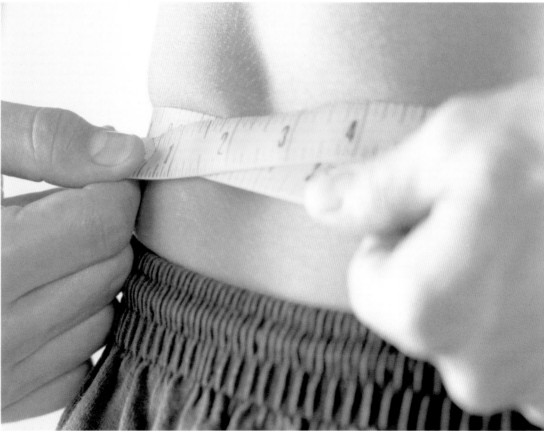

The Cholesterol Conundrum

Cholesterol occurs naturally in the body and plays a vital role in how every cell wall in the body functions. However, too much cholesterol in the blood can increase the risk of coronary heart disease. It is also a risk factor in other chronic diseases such as diabetes, stroke, and osteoporosis. Cholesterol is carried around the body in the blood on proteins called lipoproteins. A healthy body should have low levels of "bad" cholesterol (called LDL, or low-density lipoproteins) and higher levels of "good" cholesterol (called HDL, or high-density lipoproteins), as this appears to protect against coronary heart disease by removing excess cholesterol from the blood. Reducing the saturated fat content of the diet is now considered far more important than cutting down on foods in which cholesterol can be found, such as eggs, liver, and kidneys, as a way of preventing and controlling high cholesterol levels in the blood.

meat. They are also found in a few vegetable oils such as coconut and palm oil, hard margarines, and lard, and are "hidden" in processed foods like cookies, cakes, and chocolate.

Unsaturated fats can be either polyunsaturated or monounsaturated, and both play an important role in a healthy diet to replace saturated oils and help to reduce blood cholesterol levels. There are two types of polyunsaturated fats. The first is found in the seeds of plants such as the sunflower-seed and soy oil and is called omega-6. The second type comes mainly from oily fish and is called omega-3 (see page 9). Monounsaturated fats have been found to lower the amount of bad cholesterol in the blood, so they help to maintain a healthy balance of cholesterol in the body. Monounsaturated fats can be found mainly in olive oil, avocados, and nuts, all of which have been used in the recipes in the book. Recipes that are traditionally high in fat have been made with a reduced-fat content and saturated fats have been replaced with polyunsaturated or monounsaturated fats where possible.

How to Reduce Fat Intake

The recipes in the book illustrate the following ways in which you can reduce the amount of saturated fat in your diet:

1. Cut off all visible fat from meats and poultry and remove and discard any skin.
2. Use lowfat rather than whole forms of plain yogurt, mascarpone cheese, cottage cheese, and Quark.
3. Don't sauté foods in butter or lard—try to avoid sautéing foods altogether. If you have to sauté foods, use olive or corn oil instead and as little of it as possible.
4. Use skim or semiskim milk.
5. Use sauces made only with cornstarch as the thickener rather than using the traditional roux (butter and flour) method. Add flavor by using herbs, spices, and other ingredients such as fruit rind and juice.
6. Use healthier, lowfat cooking methods such as broiling and simmering rather than deep-frying.
7. Use lowfat salad dressings instead of high-fat salad creams and mayonnaise.
8. Replace butter with a spread labeled high in polyunsaturates such as a spread made with corn oil.

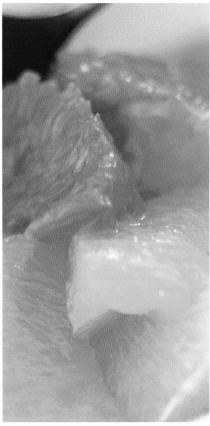

Eat More Starch and Fiber

Healthy eating recommendations advise us all to eat more starchy foods and fiber. Insoluble fiber from cereals prevents constipation and enables the digestive tract to rid the body of waste, as well as stopping cholesterol being reabsorbed into the bloodstream. Soluble fiber from fruit, beans, and vegetables can help to reduce the amount of cholesterol in the blood. Therefore, it is important to eat a varied diet so that you get the benefits of both insoluble and soluble fiber.

Breads, potatoes, pasta, and rice are starchy foods with a useful amount of fiber. These foods are good at filling us up, provide important nutrients and, because they take longer to digest, (particularly whole-grain foods) make us feel fuller for longer, which in turn can prevent us from snacking on high-fat and salty foods. If you are trying to lose weight, you should still include some starchy foods in your diet.

The recipes in this book recommend the use of brown rice, whole-wheat bread, and whole-wheat flour. However, if you are not used to eating these, introduce them gradually. It is better to eat more white bread, pasta, and rice to replace the calories lost by reducing the fat content of your diet, and they provide useful amounts of protein, vitamins, and minerals.

The Trans-fatty Acids Issue

Recently, there has been concern that the process called hydrogenation, in which various vegetable and animal oils are turned into solids to make margarine or spreads, leads to the formation of trans-fatty acids. These trans-fatty acids are treated in the body in the same way as saturated fats and so may raise the level of cholesterol in the diet if eaten in large quantities. Currently, we are advised to use a fat low in saturated fat and containing higher levels of polyunsaturated or monounsaturated fats. If possible, look carefully at the nutritional labeling and choose a product whose trans-fatty acids and saturated fat levels are less than 15 percent. For recipes in the book that require a spread rather than an oil, use a corn oil spread labeled high in polyunsaturates.

Eat More Fruit and Vegetables

Eating at least five portions of fruit and vegetables a day is recommended for a healthy diet and is also thought to help reduce the risk of coronary heart disease. Most people in the US, however, eat fewer servings that this each day, so this is an area of our health we can improve upon. Fruit and vegetables contain important antioxidants found in vitamins and these are believed to help prevent the thickening of the artery walls. Vitamins C and E are also thought to be good at aiding arterial repair. Apples, apricots, broccoli, carrots, all citrus fruits, kiwifruit, mangoes, onions, peppers, potatoes, and tomatoes are all good sources of antioxidants and have been used in many of the recipes in this book. Fruit and vegetables are also a good source of the mineral potassium, which is thought to help control blood pressure and prevent irregular heart rhythms. Bananas and potatoes are good sources of potassium and are featured in the recipes.

How to Eat Five Portions a Day

Fresh, frozen, or canned fruit and vegetables are all beneficial. Try to eat a wide selection of both fruit and vegetables. Remember that potatoes don't count as one of the five portions as they are considered a starchy food and that a glass of fruit juice counts as only one portion, no matter how much you drink. Using the recipes in this book will help you to reach the five portions a day quota. Plenty of fruit, vegetables, and salads have been included either in the recipes or suggested as accompaniments to a meal.

How big is a portion? The list below gives a general idea of amounts required to constitute one portion:

- 1 apple, orange, or banana.
- 2 plums, apricots, kiwifruit, or satsuma oranges.
- A handful of grapes, strawberries, or other small fruits.
- 2 tablespoons of vegetables.
- A small handful of dried fruit such as cranberries, raisins, or golden raisins.
- A dessert bowl of salad ingredients.
- A glass of fruit juice (about ¼ cup).

Eat More Fish

It has always been said that fish is good for you. Now, eating oily fish is actively being promoted as it is believed to play a vital role in reducing the risk of coronary heart disease. It is thought that eating oily fish may help to keep levels of the fatty substances in the blood called triglycerides down and so help prevent blood clots from forming in the arteries. Omega-3 is found in oily fish such as kippered herrings, mackerel, tuna, salmon, sardines, and pilchard. Recipes in this book like Quick Mackerel Pâté (see page 38), Teriyaki Salmon Fillets with Chinese Noodles (see page 54), Broiled Tuna & Vegetable Kabobs (see page 51), and Kipper Kedgeree (see page 26) offer tasty ways in which to enjoy oily fish. It is recommended that we eat fish two to three times a week, of which one should be oily fish.

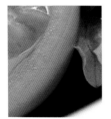

Eat Less Salt

A high consumption of salt in the diet is linked to high blood pressure. It is the sodium in salt that contributes to high blood pressure. The recommended maximum daily intake is about 2,400mg of sodium (1 teaspoon of salt), but healthy people need less than a quarter of a teaspoon of salt daily.

Most of us should try and reduce the amount of salt we eat. The recipes in this book have no salt added during the preparation or cooking of the dish. If, once you have tasted them, you feel that they need seasoning, add salt at the table, and try to reduce the amount needed gradually. Your taste buds will soon become accustomed to a lower salt content. Herbs, spices, freshly ground black pepper, and other ingredients such as lemon rind have been added to the dishes to create flavor instead of using salt. Remember if you are using manufactured foods salt will have already been added, so try not to add any more! About three-quarters of the salt we eat comes from processed foods such as bouillon cubes, cookies, ready-prepared meals, and snacks.

Eat Less Sugar

Sugar provides calories alone and no essential nutrients, and healthy eating recommendations advise that most of us should be eating less sugar. Sugar that is not used for energy is converted into fat by the liver and stored, adding to obesity and heart disease risk. The recipes in this cookbook are low in added sugar and often use the natural sugars found in fruit such as apples and dried fruit to sweeten the food. Using fruit also helps to meet the recommended five-a-day fruit and vegetable portions and provides useful amounts of fiber, vitamins, and minerals.

Drink Less Alcohol

Excessive alcohol consumption can increase blood pressure, damage the heart muscle, and lead to unwanted weight gain because alcohol provides calories with no nutritional content. Drinking alcohol is also thought to cause the platelets in the blood to become stickier, making the blood thicker, and thus hampering the blood's movement through the blood vessels.

Although excessive drinking of alcohol is not recommended, drinking in moderation may lower the risk of coronary heart disease particularly in men over 45 years of age and women over 55 years of age. Moderate consumption provides little, if any benefit, for younger people. "Moderation" means no more than one drink a day for women and no more than two per day for men, based on differences in weight and metabolism. One drink counts as 12 ounces of regular beer, 5 ounces of wine, or 1.5 ounces of distilled spirits. Consuming drinks with meals slows alcohol absorbtion. So the advice is, if you choose to drink, do so in moderation. Pregnant women are advised not to drink any alcohol at all.

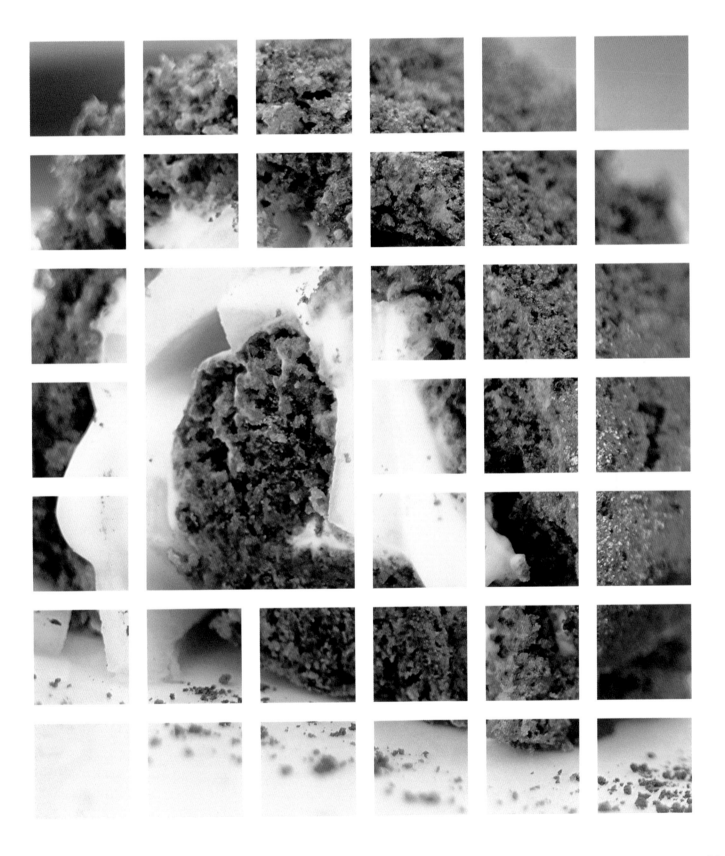

Other Lifestyle Changes for a Healthy Heart

Reduce Stress: Learn to Relax and Exercise More

Continual stress is bad for your heart as it increases the level of epinephrine in the blood. This in turn makes the blood thicker and stickier and can eventually cause the arteries to narrow and thicken. Continual stress may also cause high blood pressure. Therefore, it is very important that you find time each day to relax and unwind. Exercising can be a good way to calm down and is also beneficial to your health. We should be doing three hours' exercise a week, such as a good brisk walk, swimming, cycling, dancing, or playing a sport. Remember to take things gradually at first if you are not used to physical activity and consult a doctor if you have any health concerns before starting an exercise program.

Stop Smoking

Smoking is bad for you, and you know it, so the best thing you can do for your health is to stop. Generally people who smoke cigarettes have twice the risk of having a heart attack than nonsmokers since it contributes to the building up of fatty deposits in the arteries.

Reduce Your Risk

Remember—it is never too late to start caring for your heart and your health. The four most important steps you can take to help reduce your risk of coronary heart disease are:

1. Reduce your saturated and trans-fat intake.
2. Exercise more.
3. Eat more fruit and vegetables.
4. Stop smoking.

Breakfasts & Brunches

Breakfast is the first and most important meal of the day. Eating a healthy breakfast kick-starts your metabolism, gives you energy, and improves your concentration. Missing out on this meal can lead to hunger pangs and unhealthy high-fat and sugar-laden snacks later on. The recipes in this chapter include fast breakfasts for those who have to get up and go, as well as some ideas for more leisurely brunches for when you have time to treat yourself.

    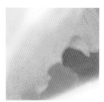 

makes 10

Cranberry Muffins

Ingredients

scant 1 1/4 cups self-rising white flour

scant 1/2 cup self-rising whole-wheat flour

1 tsp ground cinnamon

1/2 tsp baking soda

1 egg, beaten

scant 1/4 cup thin-cut orange marmalade

2/3 cup skim or semiskim milk

5 tbsp corn oil

4 oz/115 g peeled, cored, and finely diced eating apple

2/3 cup fresh or frozen cranberries, thawed if frozen

1 tbsp rolled oats

freshly squeezed orange juice, to serve

1 Preheat the oven to 400°F/200°C. Line a muffin pan with 10 muffin paper cases.

2 Put the two flours, cinnamon, and baking soda into a mixing bowl and combine thoroughly.

3 Make a well in the center of the flour mixture. In a separate bowl, blend the egg with the marmalade until well combined. Beat the milk and oil into the egg mixture, then pour into the dry ingredients, stirring lightly. Do not overmix—the batter should be slightly lumpy. Quickly stir in the apple and cranberries.

4 Spoon the batter evenly into the paper cases and sprinkle the oats over each muffin. Bake in the preheated oven for 20–25 minutes, or until well risen and golden, and a skewer inserted into the center of a muffin comes out clean.

5 Lift out the muffins and transfer onto a wire rack. Let stand for 5–10 minutes, or until slightly cooled. Peel off the paper cases and serve warm with glasses of freshly squeezed orange juice. These muffins are best eaten on the day they are made—any leftover muffins should be stored in an airtight container and consumed within 24 hours.

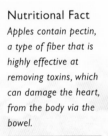

Nutritional Fact
Apples contain pectin, a type of fiber that is highly effective at removing toxins, which can damage the heart, from the body via the bowel.

Serving Analysis

• Calories	188
• Protein	4g
• Carbohydrate	25g
• Sugars	6.6g
• Fat	8.3g
• Saturates	1.4g

serves 1

Banana & Strawberry Smoothie

Ingredients

1 banana, sliced

$^{1}/_{2}$ cup fresh strawberries, hulled

generous $^{2}/_{3}$ cup lowfat plain yogurt

Nutritional Fact
Bananas contain potassium and strawberries contain antioxidants—both may help to protect the heart.

Serving Analysis

- Calories   169
- Protein   4.7g
- Carbohydrate   36.2g
- Sugars   30g
- Fat   1.95g
- Saturates   0.8g

1 Put the banana, strawberries, and yogurt into a blender and process for a few seconds until smooth.

2 Pour into a glass and serve at once.

serves 4

Exotic Dried Fruit Compote

Ingredients

generous ¹/₂ cup no-soak dried peaches

¹/₂ cup no-soak dried apricots

¹/₃ cup no-soak dried pineapple chunks

2 oz/55 g no-soak dried mango slices

1 cup unsweetened clear apple juice

4 tbsp lowfat plain yogurt (optional)

1 Put the dried fruit into a small pan with the apple juice. Bring slowly to a boil, then reduce the heat to low, cover, and let simmer for 10 minutes.

2 Spoon into serving dishes and top each serving with a tablespoon of yogurt, if desired. Serve at once.

Nutritional Fact

The fruit content here provides a great amount of soluble fiber and therefore cleans out the bowel, which is important for regulating cholesterol.

Serving Analysis

- *Calories*   165
- *Protein*   2g
- *Carbohydrate*   42g
- *Sugars*   36.6g
- *Fat*   0.49g
- *Saturates*   0.06g

serves 4

Bacon Buns

Ingredients

8 low-salt lean smoked Canadian bacon slices

6 tomatoes

1 ¹/₈ cups lowfat plain cottage cheese

freshly ground black pepper

4 large seeded whole-wheat or white bread rolls

2 scallions, chopped

1 Preheat the broiler to high. Remove any visible fat and rind from the bacon and cut 4 of the tomatoes in half. Place the bacon and tomatoes, cut-side up, under the preheated broiler and cook, turning the bacon over halfway through, for 8–10 minutes, or until the bacon is crisp and the tomatoes are softened. Remove the tomatoes and bacon from the broiler and drain the bacon on paper towels to help remove any excess fat. Keep the bacon and tomatoes warm.

2 Meanwhile, cut the remaining tomatoes into bite-size pieces and combine with the cottage cheese in a bowl. Cut the bacon into bite-size pieces and stir into the cottage cheese mixture. Season to taste with pepper.

3 Cut the bread rolls in half and divide the bacon filling evenly over each roll base. Sprinkle the scallions over the filling and cover with the roll tops. Serve at once with the broiled tomatoes.

Nutritional Fact
Tomatoes contain a substance called lycopene, which gives them their lovely red color and has great antioxidant and protective properties for the heart.

Serving Analysis
- *Calories*   *216*
- *Protein*   *16g*
- *Carbohydrate*   *21.3g*
- *Sugars*   *7.2g*
- *Fat*   *8.2g*
- *Saturates*   *3.4g*

serves 2

Melon & Kiwifruit Bowl

Ingredients

1 small charentais, cantaloupe, or galia melon

2 kiwifruit

Nutritional Fact

Kiwifruit is an excellent source of vitamin C, which is an antioxidant thought to play a key role in preventing heart disease.

Serving Analysis

- *Calories*   236
- *Protein*   3.25g
- *Carbohydrate*   54g
- *Sugars*   51g
- *Fat*   0.8g
- *Saturates*   0.14g

1 Cut the melon into quarters and remove and discard the seeds. Remove the melon flesh from the skin with a sharp knife and cut into chunks. If you have a melon baller, scoop out as much of the melon flesh as possible and place in a bowl.

2 Peel the kiwifruit and cut the flesh into slices. Add to the melon, and gently mix together. Cover and let chill until required or divide between 2 serving dishes and serve at once.

serves 1

Rise & Shine Juice

Ingredients

4 tomatoes, quartered

scant $^1/_2$ cup grated carrot

1 tbsp lime juice

Nutritional Fact
Carrots contain high amounts of beta-carotene, which gives them their vibrant orange color and their heart-protective properties.

Serving Analysis
- *Calories*   144
- *Protein*   5.1g
- *Carbohydrate*   33g
- *Sugars*   20g
- *Fat*   1.8g
- *Saturates*   0.25g

1 Put the tomatoes, carrot, and lime juice into a blender and process for a few seconds until smooth.

2 Place a nylon strainer over a bowl and pour in the tomato mixture. Using a spoon, gently push as much of the liquid through the strainer as possible. Discard any pips and pulp remaining in the strainer.

3 Pour the juice into a glass and serve at once.

serves 4

Kipper Kedgeree

Ingredients

I tbsp olive oil
2 shallots, sliced
I tsp ground cumin
I tsp ground turmeric
2 cups easy-cook brown rice
3 cups vegetable stock
2 eggs
I cup frozen peas
4 scallions, chopped
12 oz/350 g kippered herring fillets
freshly ground black pepper
2 tbsp chopped fresh parsley
lemon wedges, to garnish

1 Heat the oil in a large, heavy-bottom skillet over medium–low heat. Add the shallots, cumin, and turmeric, and cook, stirring constantly, for 1–2 minutes, or until the shallots have softened, taking care not to burn the spices as they are cooking in a small amount of oil.

2 Add the rice and stir to coat with the oil and spices. Pour in the stock and bring to a boil, then reduce the heat, cover, and simmer, stirring occasionally, for 25 minutes.

3 Meanwhile, place the eggs in a small pan of cold water and bring to a boil, then reduce the heat and let simmer for 10 minutes. Carefully remove the eggs from the hot water and place in a bowl of cold water for a few minutes. When cool enough to handle, remove, and discard the eggshells. Chop the eggs into bite-size pieces and set aside.

4 Stir the peas and scallions into the rice and return to a boil. Reduce the heat, cover, and let simmer for an additional 5 minutes.

5 Using a sharp knife, remove and discard the skin from the kippered herring fillets. Cut the fish into bite-size pieces, removing any remaining bones, and stir into the rice mixture. Return the rice to a boil, then reduce the heat, cover, and let simmer for 3–5 minutes, or until the fish is cooked, the rice is tender, and the stock has been completely absorbed. Season to taste with pepper.

6 Transfer the kedgeree to a warmed serving dish and lightly fork in the eggs. Sprinkle over the parsley, garnish with lemon wedges, and serve at once.

Nutritional Fact

Kippers are an oily fish and so contain omega-3 oils that protect the heart. It is currently recommended that you eat 2–3 portions of fish per week, one of which should be oily.

Serving Analysis

• Calories	403
• Protein	29g
• Carbo	30g
• Sugars	2.8g
• Fat	18g
• Saturates	3.4g

serves 4

Citrus Zing

Ingredients

| 1 pink grapefruit |
| 1 yellow grapefruit |
| 3 oranges |

1 Using a sharp knife, carefully cut away all the peel and pith from the grapefruit and oranges.

2 Working over a bowl to catch the juice, carefully cut the grapefruit and orange segments between the membranes to obtain skinless segments of fruit. Discard any pips. Add the segments to the bowl and gently mix together. Cover and let chill until required or divide between 4 serving dishes and serve at once.

Nutritional Fact

Citrus fruits are one of the highest sources of vitamin C, which is crucial for heart health because it is important for the healing of blood vessels.

Serving Analysis

- Calories   83
- Protein   1.6g
- Carbohydrate   21g
- Sugars   17g
- Fat   0.23g
- Saturates   0.03g

Soups & Light Meals

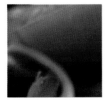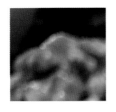

These tasty light meals are quick and easy to make—some are also ideal for making healthy packed lunches. They provide a filling meal and should stop you reaching for those unhealthy snacks between meals. If you do feel peckish, choose healthier snacks such as a piece of fruit, bread sticks, a currant bun, strips of vegetables with a lowfat dip, or salt- and sugar-free homemade popcorn.

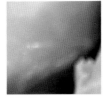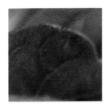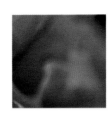

serves 6

Winter Warmer Red Lentil Soup

Ingredients

generous 1 cup dried red split lentils

1 red onion, diced

2 large carrots, sliced

1 celery stalk, sliced

1 parsnip, diced

1 garlic clove, crushed

5 cups vegetable stock

2 tsp paprika

freshly ground black pepper

1 tbsp snipped fresh chives, to garnish

To serve

6 tbsp lowfat plain mascarpone cheese (optional)

crusty whole-wheat or white bread

Nutritional Fact

Lentils contain good levels of B vitamins, which are thought to stop the buildup of a substance called homocysteine that can build up in the body and cause damage to the heart.

Serving Analysis

- Calories   87
- Protein   4.4g
- Carbohydrate   18g
- Sugars   5g
- Fat   0.4g
- Saturates   0.07g

1 Put the lentils, onion, vegetables, garlic, stock, and paprika into a large pan. Bring to a boil and boil rapidly for 10 minutes. Reduce the heat, cover, and let simmer for 20 minutes, or until the lentils and vegetables are tender.

2 Let the soup cool slightly, then purée in small batches in a food processor or blender. Process until the mixture is smooth.

3 Return the soup to the pan and heat through thoroughly. Season to taste with pepper.

4 To serve, ladle the soup into warmed bowls and swirl in a tablespoonful of mascarpone cheese, if desired. Sprinkle the chives over the soup to garnish and serve at once with crusty bread.

serves 6

Speedy Broccoli Soup

Ingredients

12 oz/350 g broccoli
1 leek, sliced
1 celery stalk, sliced
1 garlic clove, crushed
12 oz/350 g potato, diced
4 cups vegetable stock
1 bay leaf
freshly ground black pepper
crusty bread or toasted croutons, to serve

Nutritional Fact

Broccoli is a source of vitamins B$_3$ and B$_5$, both of which are thought to raise good cholesterol levels in the blood, and therefore help to balance good and bad cholesterol levels.

Serving Analysis

- Calories   140
- Protein   5.6g
- Carbohydrate   29g
- Sugars   3.6g
- Fat   1.3g
- Saturates   0.27g

1 Cut the broccoli into florets and set aside. Cut the thicker broccoli stalks into $^1/_2$-inch/1-cm dice and put into a large pan with the leek, celery, garlic, potato, stock, and bay leaf. Bring to a boil, then reduce the heat, cover, and let simmer for 15 minutes

2 Add the broccoli florets to the soup and return to a boil. Reduce the heat, cover, and let simmer for an additional 3–5 minutes, or until the potato and broccoli stalks are tender.

3 Remove from the heat and let the soup cool slightly. Remove and discard the bay leaf. Purée the soup, in small batches, in a food processor or blender until smooth.

4 Return the soup to the pan and heat through thoroughly. Season to taste with pepper. Ladle the soup into warmed bowls and serve at once with crusty bread or toasted croutons.

serves 6

Chunky Vegetable Soup

Ingredients

2 carrots, sliced

1 onion, diced

1 garlic clove, crushed

12 oz/350 g new potatoes, diced

2 celery stalks, sliced

4 oz/115 g closed-cup mushrooms, quartered

14 oz/400 g canned chopped tomatoes in tomato juice

2¹/₂ cups vegetable stock

1 bay leaf

1 tsp dried mixed herbs or 1 tbsp chopped fresh mixed herbs

¹/₂ cup corn kernels, frozen or canned, drained

2 oz/55 g green cabbage, shredded

freshly ground black pepper

few sprigs of fresh basil, to garnish (optional)

crusty whole-wheat or white bread rolls, to serve

Nutritional Fact
This dish can help you to achieve the target of five portions of fruit and vegetables you should aim for daily, which is crucial to a healthy heart.

Serving Analysis
- Calories — 179
- Protein — 5.4g
- Carbohydrate — 34g
- Sugars — 6g
- Fat — 1.7g
- Saturates — 0.07g

1 Put the carrots, onion, garlic, potatoes, celery, mushrooms, tomatoes, and stock into a large pan. Stir in the bay leaf and herbs. Bring to a boil, then reduce the heat, cover, and let simmer for 25 minutes.

2 Add the corn and cabbage and return to a boil. Reduce the heat, cover, and let simmer for 5 minutes, or until the vegetables are tender. Remove and discard the bay leaf. Season to taste with pepper.

3 Ladle into warmed bowls and garnish with basil. Serve at once with crusty bread rolls.

serves 4

Quick Mackerel Pâté

Ingredients

9 oz/250 g skinless smoked mackerel fillets

generous ²/₃ cup lowfat plain yogurt

1 tbsp chopped fresh parsley

1 tbsp lemon juice

finely grated rind of ¹/₂ lemon

freshly ground black pepper

To garnish

4 lemon wedges

few sprigs of fresh parsley

To serve

1 red bell pepper, seeded and cut into chunky strips

1 yellow bell pepper, seeded and cut into chunky strips

2 carrots, cut into strips

2 celery stalks, cut into strips

slices whole-wheat or white bread, toasted and cut into triangles

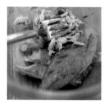

Nutritional Fact
Mackerel is an oily fish and a very rich source of omega-3 oils. These oils are excellent for helping to keep the heart healthy.

Serving Analysis
- Calories   190
- Protein   17g
- Carbohydrate   3.4g
- Sugars   2.9g
- Fat   11.7g
- Saturates   2.9g

1 Remove and discard any remaining bones from the mackerel fillets and put the fish into a small bowl. Mash the fish with a fork and combine with the yogurt, parsley, and lemon juice and rind. Season to taste with pepper.

2 Divide the pâté between 4 ramekins. Cover and let chill until required or serve at once.

3 To serve, garnish the pâté with lemon wedges and parsley sprigs and serve with the prepared vegetables and toasted bread.

serves 4

Raisin Coleslaw & Tuna-Filled Pita Breads

Ingredients

scant ¹/₂ cup grated carrot

2 oz/55 g white cabbage, thinly sliced

¹/₃ cup lowfat plain yogurt

1 tsp cider vinegar

generous ¹/₈ cup raisins

7 oz/200 g canned tuna steak in water, drained

2 tbsp pepitas

freshly ground black pepper

4 whole-wheat or white pita breads

4 eating apples, to serve

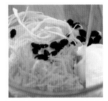

Nutritional Fact
Pepitas contain omega-3 oils and omega-6 oils, both of which are thought to be beneficial to the heart.

Serving Analysis
- *Calories*   351
- *Protein*   21g
- *Carbohydrate*   59g
- *Sugars*   21g
- *Fat*   5.3g
- *Saturates*   1.6g

1 Mix the carrot, cabbage, yogurt, vinegar, and raisins together in a bowl. Lightly stir in the tuna and half the pepitas and season to taste with pepper.

2 Lightly toast the pita breads under a preheated hot broiler or in a toaster, then let cool slightly. Using a sharp knife, cut each pita bread in half. Divide the filling evenly between the pita breads and sprinkle the remaining pepitas over the filling. Core and cut the apples into wedges, then serve at once with the filled pita breads.

serves 4

Salmon & Avocado Salad

Ingredients

1 lb/450 g new potatoes

4 salmon steaks, about 4 oz/
115 g each

1 avocado

juice of ¹/₂ lemon

1¹/₄ cups baby spinach leaves

4¹/₂ oz/125 g mixed small salad greens,
including watercress

12 cherry tomatoes, halved

scant ¹/₂ cup chopped walnuts

For the dressing

3 tbsp unsweetened clear apple juice

1 tsp balsamic vinegar

freshly ground black pepper

1 Cut the new potatoes into bite-size pieces, put into a pan, and cover with cold water. Bring to a boil, then reduce the heat, cover, and let simmer for 10–15 minutes, or until just tender. Drain and keep warm.

2 Meanwhile, preheat the broiler to medium. Cook the salmon steaks under the preheated broiler for 10–15 minutes, depending on the thickness of the steaks, turning halfway through cooking. Remove from the broiler and keep warm.

3 While the potatoes and salmon are cooking, cut the avocado in half, remove and discard the pit, and peel the flesh. Cut the avocado flesh into slices and coat in the lemon juice to prevent it discoloring.

4 Toss the spinach leaves and mixed salad greens together in a large serving bowl until combined. Arrange 6 cherry tomato halves on each plate of salad.

5 Remove and discard the skin and any bones from the salmon. Flake the salmon and divide between the plates along with the potatoes. Sprinkle the walnuts over the salads.

6 To make the dressing, mix the apple juice and vinegar together in a small bowl or pitcher and season well with pepper. Drizzle over the salads and serve at once.

Nutritional Fact
Salmon contains beneficial omega-3 oils and avocado has good levels of soluble fiber and beneficial fats that protect the heart.

Serving Analysis

- *Calories*   *432*
- *Protein*   *29g*
- *Carbohydrate*   *34g*
- *Sugars*   *4.5g*
- *Fat*   *21g*
- *Saturates*   *2.1g*

Fish, Meat & Poultry

Using lean cuts of meat, removing the skin from poultry, and increasing our consumption of fish are good ways to reduce the saturated fat content of our meals without compromising on the taste. These recipes demonstrate healthier ways to cook meat and fish dishes and suggest tasty accompaniments such as pasta, noodles, rice, couscous, bread, salads, and seasonal vegetables.

    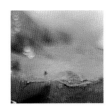 

serves 4

Smoked Haddock with Tagliatelle Verde

Ingredients

1 lb/450 g smoked haddock fillets
10 oz/280 g dried tagliatelle verde
2¹/₂ cups skim or semiskim milk
4 tbsp cornstarch
2 shallots, finely chopped
2 tbsp snipped fresh chives
freshly ground black pepper
sliced tomatoes, to serve

1 Using a sharp knife, remove and discard the skin from the haddock fillets. Cut the fish into chunks, removing any remaining bones.

2 Bring a large pan of water to a boil, add the tagliatelle, and return to a boil. Cook for 8–10 minutes, or until just tender.

3 Meanwhile, blend ¹/₂ cup of the milk with the cornstarch in a heatproof 3¹/₂-cup bowl. Place the remaining milk in a pan with the shallots and bring to a boil. Pour the boiling milk over the cornstarch mixture, stirring constantly. Return the milk to the pan and return to a boil, stirring constantly, until the sauce thickens.

4 Stir the fish into the sauce, reduce the heat to low, and gently simmer for 5 minutes, or until the fish is cooked. Stir in half of the chives.

5 Drain the tagliatelle and return to the pan, stir in the haddock sauce, and season to taste with pepper. Serve at once, garnished with the remaining chives and accompanied by sliced tomatoes.

Nutritional Fact

Haddock, although not an oily fish, is an excellent source of vitamin A, which is an antioxidant nutrient and therefore protects the heart against damage.

Serving Analysis

• Calories	48
• Protein	39g
• Carbohydrate	48g
• Sugars	6.7g
• Fat	12g
• Saturates	4.5g

serves 4

Broiled Tuna & Vegetable Kabobs

Ingredients

4 tuna steaks, about 5 oz/140 g each

2 red onions

12 cherry tomatoes

1 red bell pepper, seeded and diced into 1-inch/2.5-cm pieces

1 yellow bell pepper, seeded and diced into 1-inch/2.5-cm pieces

1 zucchini, sliced

1 tbsp chopped fresh oregano

4 tbsp olive oil

freshly ground black pepper

lime wedges, to garnish

To serve

selection of salads

cooked couscous, new potatoes, or bread

Nutritional Fact

It is important to eat many different fruit and vegetables to provide good levels of potassium to help lower high blood pressure and prevent heart disease.

Serving Analysis

- *Calories*   *371*
- *Protein*   *35g*
- *Carbohydrate*   *15g*
- *Sugars*   *7.7g*
- *Fat*   *20g*
- *Saturates*   *0.08g*

1 Preheat the broiler to high. Cut the tuna into 1-inch/2.5-cm dice. Peel the onions, leaving the root intact, and cut each onion lengthwise into 6 wedges.

2 Divide the fish and vegetables evenly between 8 wooden skewers (presoaked to avoid burning) and arrange on the broiler pan.

3 Mix the oregano and oil together in a small bowl. Season to taste with pepper. Lightly brush the kabobs with the oil and cook under the preheated broiler for 10–15 minutes or until evenly cooked, turning occasionally. If you cannot fit all the kabobs on the broiler pan at once, cook them in batches, keeping the cooked kabobs warm while cooking the remainder. Alternatively, these kabobs can be cooked on a barbecue.

4 Garnish with lime wedges and serve with a selection of salads, cooked couscous, new potatoes, or bread.

serves 4

Baked Lemon Cod

Nutritional Fact

White fish, such as cod and flounder, is low in saturated fat and high in protein that is essential for healthy building and repair of the body's cells.

Serving Analysis

- *Calories*   121
- *Protein*   25g
- *Carbohydrate*   2.6g
- *Sugars*   1.2g
- *Fat*   1.3g
- *Saturates*   0.02g

Ingredients

4 oz/115 g cucumber

2 celery stalks

4 thick cod fillets, about 5 oz/140 g each

1 tbsp chopped fresh parsley

grated rind and juice of 1 lemon

freshly ground black pepper

lemon wedges, to garnish

boiled new potatoes, lightly cooked seasonal vegetables, or salads, to serve

1 Preheat the oven to 400°F/200°C. Cut the cucumber and celery into long fine sticks and sprinkle over the base of an ovenproof dish that is large enough to fit the cod fillets in a single layer.

2 Arrange the cod fillets on the cucumber and celery and sprinkle the parsley, lemon rind, and juice over the fillets. Season with pepper. Cover the dish with an ovenproof lid or foil and bake in the preheated oven for about 20 minutes, depending on the thickness of the fillets, until the flesh turns white and flakes easily.

3 Transfer the fish to a warmed serving plate with the cucumber and celery and spoon over the cooking juices. Garnish with lemon wedges and serve at once with boiled new potatoes, seasonal vegetables, or salads.

serves 4

Teriyaki Salmon Fillets with Chinese Noodles

Ingredients

4 salmon fillets, about 7 oz/200 g each

$^1/_2$ cup teriyaki marinade

1 shallot, sliced

$^3/_4$-inch/2-cm piece fresh gingerroot, finely chopped

2 carrots, sliced

4 oz/115 g closed-cup mushrooms, sliced

5 cups vegetable stock

9 oz/250 g dried medium egg noodles

1 cup frozen peas

6 oz/175 g Napa cabbage, shredded

4 scallions, sliced

1 Wipe off any fish scales from the salmon skin. Arrange the salmon fillets, skin-side up, in a dish just large enough to fit them in a single layer. Mix the teriyaki marinade with the shallot and ginger in a small bowl and pour over the salmon. Cover and let marinate in the refrigerator for at least 1 hour, turning the salmon over halfway through the marinating time.

2 Put the carrots, mushrooms, and stock into a large pan. Arrange the salmon, skin-side down, on a shallow baking sheet. Pour the fish marinade into the pan of vegetables and stock and bring to a boil. Reduce the heat, cover, and let simmer for 10 minutes.

3 Meanwhile, preheat the broiler to medium. Cook the salmon under the preheated broiler for 10–15 minutes, depending on the thickness of the fillets, until the flesh turns pink and flakes easily. Remove from the broiler and keep warm.

4 Add the noodles and peas to the stock and return to a boil. Reduce the heat, cover, and let simmer for 5 minutes, or until the noodles are tender. Stir in the Napa cabbage and scallions and heat through for 1 minute.

5 Carefully drain off 1¼ cups of the stock into a small heatproof pitcher and set aside. Drain and discard the remaining stock. Divide the noodles and vegetables between 4 warmed serving bowls and top each with a salmon fillet. Pour the reserved stock over each meal and serve at once.

Nutritional Fact

Peas are legumes, not vegetables, and provide good protective levels of B vitamins and soluble fiber; they even retain these when frozen.

Serving Analysis

- Calories   533
- Protein   49g
- Carbohydrate   34.7g
- Sugars   13g
- Fat   22.4g
- Saturates   5.7g

serves 4

Boeuf Bourguignonne

Ingredients

14 oz/400 g lean beef

2 low-salt lean smoked Canadian bacon slices

12 shallots, peeled

1 garlic clove, crushed

8 oz/225 g closed-cap mushrooms, sliced

1 1/4 cups red wine

scant 2 cups beef stock

2 bay leaves

2 tbsp chopped fresh thyme

3/8 cup cornstarch

generous 1/3 cup cold water

freshly ground black pepper

To serve

boiled brown or white rice

lightly cooked seasonal vegetables

Nutritional Fact

Choosing brown rice instead of white can help to increase your intake of insoluble fiber and B vitamins and clean toxins out of your system.

Serving Analysis

• Calories	376
• Protein	35g
• Carbohydrate	20g
• Sugars	1.6g
• Fat	11g
• Saturates	4.1g

1 Trim any visible fat from the beef and bacon and cut the meat into bite-size pieces. Put the meat into a large pan with the shallots, garlic, mushrooms, wine, stock, bay leaves, and 1 tablespoon of the thyme. Bring to a boil, then reduce the heat, cover, and let simmer for 50 minutes, or until the meat and shallots are tender.

2 Blend the cornstarch with the water in a small bowl and stir into the casserole. Return to a boil, stirring constantly, and cook until the casserole thickens. Reduce the heat and let simmer for an additional 5 minutes. Season to taste with pepper.

3 Remove and discard the bay leaves. Transfer the boeuf bourguignonne to a warmed casserole dish and sprinkle over the remaining thyme. Serve with boiled rice and seasonal vegetables.

serves 4

Moroccan-Style Turkey with Apricots

1 Put the turkey, onion, cumin, cinnamon, chili pepper sauce, chickpeas, and stock into a large pan and bring to a boil, then reduce the heat, cover, and let simmer for 15 minutes.

2 Stir in the apricots and return to a boil. Reduce the heat, cover, and let simmer for an additional 15 minutes, or until the turkey is thoroughly cooked and tender.

3 Blend the cornstarch with the water in a small bowl and stir into the casserole. Return to a boil, stirring constantly, and cook until the casserole thickens. Reduce the heat, cover, and let simmer for an additional 5 minutes.

4 Stir half the cilantro into the casserole. Transfer to a warmed serving dish and sprinkle over the remaining cilantro. Serve at once with cooked couscous, rice, or baked sweet potatoes.

Nutritional Fact
Cumin has been traditionally used for centuries in the East as a heart tonic because it stimulates the circulation; it also helps digestion.

Serving Analysis
- Calories   387
- Protein   26g
- Carbohydrate   63g
- Sugars   36g
- Fat   4.7g
- Saturates   1.3g

Ingredients

14 oz/400 g skinless, boneless turkey breast, diced

1 onion, sliced

1 tsp ground cumin

1/2 tsp ground cinnamon

1 tsp hot chili pepper sauce

8 1/2 oz/240 g canned chickpeas, drained

2 1/2 cups chicken stock

12 dried apricots

generous 1/4 cup cornstarch

generous 1/4 cup cold water

2 tbsp chopped fresh cilantro

cooked couscous, rice, or baked sweet potatoes, to serve

serves 4

Chicken Jambalaya

Ingredients

14 oz/400 g skinless, boneless chicken breast, diced

1 red onion, diced

1 garlic clove, crushed

2 1/2 cups chicken stock

14 oz/400 g canned chopped tomatoes in tomato juice

generous 1 1/2 cups brown rice

1–2 tsp hot chili powder

1/2 tsp paprika

1 tsp dried oregano

1 red bell pepper, seeded and diced

1 yellow bell pepper, seeded and diced

1/2 cup frozen corn kernels

3/4 cup frozen peas

3 tbsp chopped fresh parsley

freshly ground black pepper

crisp green salad, to serve

Nutritional Fact

Garlic is an important ingredient for a healthy heart. Its active component, allicin, helps to stimulate circulation and keep blood thin to prevent heart disease.

Serving Analysis

- Calories 309
- Protein 34.5g
- Carbohydrate 36g
- Sugars 8.3g
- Fat 3.4g
- Saturates 0.2g

1 Put the chicken, onion, garlic, stock, tomatoes, and rice into a large, heavy-bottom pan. Add the chili powder, paprika, and oregano and stir well. Bring to a boil, then reduce the heat, cover, and let simmer for 25 minutes.

2 Add the red and yellow bell peppers, corn, and peas to the rice mixture and return to a boil. Reduce the heat, cover, and let simmer for an additional 10 minutes, or until the rice is just tender (brown rice retains a "nutty" texture when cooked) and most of the stock has been absorbed but is not completely dry.

3 Stir in 2 tablespoons of the parsley and season to taste with pepper. Transfer the jambalaya to a warmed serving dish, garnish with the remaining parsley, and serve with a crisp green salad.

serves 4

Sticky Lime Chicken

1 Preheat the oven to 375°F/190°C. Arrange the chicken breasts in a shallow roasting pan.

2 Put the lime rind and juice, honey, oil, garlic, if using, and thyme in a small bowl and combine thoroughly. Spoon the mixture evenly over the chicken breasts and season with pepper.

3 Roast the chicken in the preheated oven, basting every 10 minutes, for 35–40 minutes, or until the chicken is tender and the juices run clear when a skewer is inserted into the thickest part of the meat. If the juices still run pink, return the chicken to the oven and cook for an additional 5 minutes, then retest. As the chicken cooks, the liquid in the pan thickens to give the tasty, sticky coating.

4 Serve with boiled new potatoes and seasonal vegetables.

Ingredients

4 part-boned, skinless chicken breasts, about 5 oz/140 g each

grated rind and juice of 1 lime

1 tbsp honey

1 tbsp olive oil

1 garlic clove, chopped (optional)

1 tbsp chopped fresh thyme

freshly ground black pepper

To serve

boiled new potatoes

lightly cooked seasonal vegetables

Nutritional Fact
Removing the skin from the chicken gets rid of most of the saturated fat.

Serving Analysis
- Calories 203
- Protein 32.5g
- Carbohydrate 5.3g
- Sugars 4.4g
- Fat 5.3g
- Saturates 1g

Vegetarian

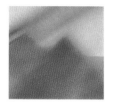 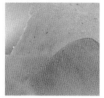 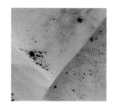  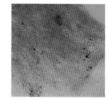 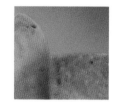

You don't have to be a vegetarian to enjoy the delicious recipes in this chapter. The variety of flavors and textures featured in the selection of vegetables available today makes a delightful change from meat-based recipes. Fresh chilies, herbs, ginger, and Asian spices are just some of the ingredients used to enhance these easy-to-make meals.

  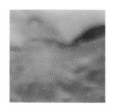 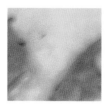 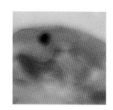 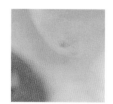

serves 4

Roasted Vegetables with Hot Chili Pepper Dip

Ingredients

4 tbsp olive oil

2 potatoes, about 6 oz/175 g each

2 red-fleshed sweet potatoes, about 6 oz/175 g each

1 large parsnip

6 turnips, about 3 oz/85 g each

few sprigs of fresh rosemary

2 garlic cloves, crushed

2 zucchini

1 eggplant

For the dip

3 fresh red chilies, sliced

1 red bell pepper, seeded and finely diced

1 onion, finely chopped

14 oz/400 g canned chopped tomatoes in tomato juice

generous $1/3$ cup vegetable stock or cold water

1 Preheat the oven to 425°F/220°C. Divide the oil between 2 large roasting pans and heat in the oven.

2 Scrub the potatoes and cut into wedges. Peel the parsnip and turnips. Cut the parsnip into strips about the same size as the potato wedges. Cut the turnips in half. Cook in a large pan of boiling water for 5 minutes, drain well, and carefully add to the roasting pans. Using a spoon, turn and coat the vegetables with the hot oil. Divide the rosemary and garlic between the roasting pans and roast in the preheated oven for 15 minutes.

3 Cut the zucchini and eggplant into long chunks, just slightly larger than the potato wedges. Remove the roasting pans from the oven and divide the zucchini and eggplant between them, carefully tossing them in the hot oil. Roast for an additional 45 minutes–1 hour, turning occasionally so that they roast evenly.

4 Meanwhile, make the dip. Set aside a few chili slices for garnish and put the remainder into a pan with all the remaining dip ingredients. Bring to a boil, then reduce the heat, cover, and let simmer for 20 minutes until the onion is tender. Let the dip cool for 15 minutes, then process in a food processor or blender in small batches, until smooth. Return the dip to the pan and heat through thoroughly just prior to serving.

5 Pour the dip into 4 individual serving dishes and garnish with the reserved chili slices. Divide the roasted vegetables between warmed serving plates. Serve at once.

Nutritional Fact

Roasting vegetables in olive oil is much healthier than using saturated lard or butter.

Serving Analysis

- *Calories*   *443*
- *Protein*   *9.7g*
- *Carbohydrate*   *74g*
- *Sugars*   *26.5g*
- *Fat*   *15g*
- *Saturates*   *0.2g*

serves 4

Mushroom Stroganoff

Ingredients

1 lb 4 oz/550 g mixed fresh mushrooms, such as cremini, chanterelles, cèpes, and oyster

1 red onion, diced

2 garlic cloves, crushed

scant 2 cups vegetable stock

1 tbsp tomato paste

2 tbsp lemon juice

scant 1 tbsp cornstarch

2 tbsp cold water

½ cup lowfat plain yogurt

3 tbsp chopped fresh parsley

freshly ground black pepper

To serve

boiled brown or white rice

crisp green salad

Nutritional Fact
Mushrooms have long been eaten to promote health and vitality and are said to enhance the body's adaptive capacity to fight disease and strengthen itself.

Serving Analysis
- *Calories*   87
- *Protein*   5.1g
- *Carbohydrate*   16.8g
- *Sugars*   4.4g
- *Fat*   1.2g
- *Saturates*   0.4g

1 Put the mushrooms, onion, garlic, stock, tomato paste, and lemon juice into a pan and bring to a boil. Reduce the heat, cover, and let simmer for 15 minutes, or until the onion is tender.

2 Blend the cornstarch with the water in a small bowl and stir into the mushroom mixture. Return to a boil, stirring constantly, and cook until the sauce thickens. Reduce the heat and let simmer for an additional 2–3 minutes, stirring occasionally.

3 Just before serving, remove the pan from the heat, and stir in the yogurt, making sure that the stroganoff is not boiling or it may separate and curdle. Stir in 2 tablespoons of the parsley and season to taste with pepper. Transfer the stroganoff to a warmed serving dish, sprinkle over the remaining parsley, and serve at once with boiled brown or white rice and a crisp green salad.

serves 4

Toasted Pine Nut & Vegetable Couscous

Ingredients

generous $^1/_2$ cup dried green lentils

$^3/_8$ cup pine nuts

1 tbsp olive oil

1 onion, diced

2 garlic cloves, crushed

10 oz/280 g zucchini, sliced

9 oz/250 g tomatoes, chopped

14 oz/400 g canned artichoke hearts, drained and cut in half lengthwise

generous 1 $^1/_4$ cups couscous

2 cups vegetable stock

3 tbsp torn fresh basil leaves, plus extra leaves to garnish

freshly ground black pepper

Nutritional Fact

Pine nuts have beneficial omega-3 oils and polyunsaturated fats. They also contain plant sterols, which are thought to help to regulate cholesterol.

Serving Analysis

• *Calories*	*600*
• *Protein*	*17g*
• *Carbohydrate*	*71g*
• *Sugars*	*7.9g*
• *Fat*	*28g*
• *Saturates*	*4g*

1 Put the lentils into a pan with plenty of cold water, bring to a boil, and boil rapidly for 10 minutes. Reduce the heat, cover, and let simmer for an additional 15 minutes, or until tender.

2 Meanwhile, preheat the broiler to medium. Spread the pine nuts out in a single layer on a baking sheet and toast under the preheated broiler, turning to brown evenly—watch constantly because they brown very quickly. Tip the pine nuts into a small dish and set aside.

3 Heat the oil in a nonstick skillet over medium heat, add the onion, garlic, and zucchini and cook, stirring frequently, for 8–10 minutes, or until tender and the zucchini have browned slightly. Add the tomatoes and artichoke halves and heat through thoroughly for 5 minutes.

4 Meanwhile, put the couscous into a heatproof bowl. Bring the stock to a boil in a pan and pour over the couscous, cover, and let stand for 10 minutes until the couscous absorbs the stock and becomes tender.

5 Drain the lentils and stir into the couscous. Stir in the torn basil leaves and season well with pepper. Transfer the couscous to a warmed serving dish and spoon over the cooked vegetables. Sprinkle the pine nuts over the top of the vegetables and couscous, garnish with basil leaves, and serve at once.

serves 4

Tomato, Zucchini & Basil Phyllo Tartlets

Nutritional Fact
Eggs contain good levels of iron, which is essential for healthy red blood cells. They also contain vitamins B_6 and B_{12}, which are thought to help prevent arteries furring up.

Serving Analysis

- *Calories* 232
- *Protein* 7g
- *Carbohydrate* 18.7g
- *Sugars* 5.8g
- *Fat* 14.8g
- *Saturates* 3.7g

1 Preheat the oven to 375°F/190°C. Lightly oil 4 x 4½-inch/12-cm individual loose-bottom tart pans.

2 Working quickly so that the phyllo pastry does not dry out, cut each sheet into 6 equal-size pieces measuring about 6¼ x 5½ inches/16 x 14 cm. Layer 3 pieces of pastry at a time in the 4 tart pans, lightly brushing between each layer with oil. Carefully press the pastry into the sides of the pans so that the corners of the pastry squares point upward. Arrange the pans on a large baking sheet.

3 Sprinkle two-thirds of the torn basil leaves over the pastry bases and cover with overlapping slices of tomato and zucchini. Beat the eggs with the milk in a bowl and season well with pepper. Divide the egg mixture evenly between the pans and sprinkle the remaining torn basil leaves over it.

4 Bake in the preheated oven for 20–25 minutes, or until the egg mixture has set and the pastry is crisp and golden. Serve warm or cold, garnished with basil leaves, and with a selection of salads and boiled new potatoes.

Ingredients

olive oil, for oiling and brushing

2 x 19- x 11-inch/48- x 28-cm sheets phyllo pastry

1 tbsp torn fresh basil leaves, plus extra leaves to garnish

7–8 cherry tomatoes, thinly sliced

1 zucchini, thinly sliced

2 eggs, beaten

⅔ cup skim or semiskim milk

freshly ground black pepper

To serve

selection of salads

boiled new potatoes

serves 4

Corn & Green Bean-Filled Baked Sweet Potatoes

Ingredients

4 red-fleshed sweet potatoes, about 9 oz/250 g each

1 cup frozen fava beans

scant ³/₄ cup frozen corn kernels

4 oz/115 g fine long green beans

5 oz/140 g tomatoes

1 tbsp olive oil

1 tbsp balsamic vinegar

freshly ground black pepper

2 tbsp torn fresh basil leaves, plus extra leaves to garnish

Nutritional Fact

Corn is one of the few vegetables that has beneficial antioxidant properties that actually increase with cooking.

Serving Analysis

- *Calories*   *362*
- *Protein*   *8g*
- *Carbohydrate*   *76g*
- *Sugars*   *28g*
- *Fat*   *4.2g*
- *Saturates*   *0.1g*

1 Preheat the oven to 375°F/190°C. Scrub the sweet potatoes and pierce the skin of each potato with a sharp knife several times. Arrange on a baking sheet and bake in the preheated oven for 1–1¹/₄ hours, or until soft and tender when pierced with the point of a sharp knife. Keep warm.

2 When the potatoes are cooked, bring a pan of water to a boil, add the fava beans and corn, and return to a boil. Reduce the heat, cover, and let simmer for 5 minutes. Trim the green beans, cut in half, and add to the pan. Return to a boil, then reduce the heat, cover, and let simmer for 3 minutes, or until the green beans are just tender.

3 Blend the oil with the vinegar in a small bowl and season to taste with pepper. Drain the corn and beans, return to the pan, add the tomatoes, and pour the dressing over. Add the torn basil leaves and mix well.

4 Remove the sweet potatoes from the oven, cut in half lengthwise, and open up. Divide the corn and bean filling between the potatoes and serve at once, garnished with basil leaves.

serves 4–6

Chili Beans

Ingredients

7 oz/200 g dried mixed beans, such as kidney, soy, pinto, cannellini, and chickpeas

1 red onion, diced

1 garlic clove, crushed

1 tbsp hot chili powder

14 oz/400 g canned chopped tomatoes in tomato juice

1 tbsp tomato paste

To serve

4 tbsp lowfat plain yogurt

baked potatoes, boiled rice, or soft flour tortilla wraps

Nutritional Fact
Cooking tomatoes actually increases the antioxidant activity of a substance called lycopene, which gives them their color and protects the heart.

Serving Analysis
- *Calories*   53
- *Protein*   3.2g
- *Carbohydrate*   10g
- *Sugars*   4.3g
- *Fat*   0.5g
- *Saturates*   0.05g

1 Soak the beans overnight or for 8 hours in a large bowl of cold water. Drain, rinse, and put the beans into a large pan. Cover well with cold water, then bring to a boil and boil rapidly for 10 minutes. Reduce the heat, cover, and let simmer for an additional 45 minutes, or until tender. Drain. (Alternatively, if time is short, use 1 lb/450 g drained and rinsed canned mixed beans and start at Step 2.)

2 Put the cooked beans, onion, garlic, chili powder, tomatoes, and tomato paste into a pan and bring to a boil. Reduce the heat, cover, and let simmer for 20–25 minutes, or until the onion is tender.

3 Serve each portion of the chili beans with a tablespoon of the yogurt, accompanied by baked potatoes, boiled rice, or soft flour tortilla wraps.

serves 4

Curried Potato, Cauliflower & Spinach

Ingredients

2 tbsp olive oil

I onion, diced

I tbsp garam masala

$^1/_2$ tsp ground cumin

I tsp ground turmeric

14 oz/400 g canned chopped tomatoes in tomato juice

I $^1/_4$ cups vegetable stock

I lb/450 g new potatoes, cut into chunks

10 oz/280 g cauliflower florets

$^1/_2$ cup slivered almonds

5$^5/_8$ cups baby spinach leaves

naan bread, to serve

I Heat the oil in a pan over medium–low heat, add the onion and spices, and cook, stirring constantly, for 2–3 minutes, taking care not to burn the spices as they are cooking in a small amount of oil. Add the tomatoes and stock and bring to a boil, then reduce the heat, cover, and let simmer for 25 minutes.

2 Meanwhile, put the potatoes into a separate pan, cover with cold water, and bring to a boil. Reduce the heat, cover, and let simmer for 15 minutes. Add the cauliflower and return to a boil, then reduce the heat, cover, and let simmer for an additional 10 minutes, or until just tender.

3 While the vegetables are cooking, preheat the broiler to medium. Spread the almonds out in a single layer on a baking sheet and toast under the preheated broiler, turning to brown evenly, for 1–2 minutes—watch constantly because they brown very quickly. Tip the almonds into a small dish and set aside.

4 Add the spinach to the potatoes and cauliflower, stir into the water, and let simmer for I minute. Drain the vegetables and return to the pan. Stir in the curried tomato sauce. Transfer to a warmed serving dish, sprinkle over the toasted almonds, and serve at once with naan bread.

Nutritional Fact

Turmeric has been shown to lower cholesterol, prevent the formation of internal blood clots, improve circulation, and may help to prevent heart disease and strokes.

Serving Analysis
- *Calories*   339
- *Protein*   11g
- *Carbohydrate*   43g
- *Sugars*   6.6g
- *Fat*   15.6g
- *Saturates*   1.7g

serves 4

Chinese Vegetables with Noodles

Ingredients

5 cups vegetable stock

1 garlic clove, crushed

$^{1}/_{2}$-inch/1-cm piece fresh gingerroot, finely chopped

8 oz/225 g dried medium egg noodles

1 red bell pepper, seeded and sliced

$^{3}/_{4}$ cup frozen peas

4 oz/115 g broccoli florets

3 oz/85 g shiitake mushrooms, sliced

2 tbsp sesame seeds

8 oz/225 g canned water chestnuts, drained and halved

8 oz/225 g canned bamboo shoots, drained

10 oz/280 g Napa cabbage, sliced

scant 1 cup bean sprouts

3 scallions, sliced

1 tbsp dark soy sauce

freshly ground black pepper

1 Bring the stock, garlic, and ginger to a boil in a large pan. Stir in the noodles, red bell pepper, peas, broccoli, and mushrooms and return to a boil. Reduce the heat, cover, and let simmer for 5–6 minutes, or until the noodles are tender.

2 Meanwhile, preheat the broiler to medium. Spread the sesame seeds out in a single layer on a baking sheet and toast under the preheated broiler, turning to brown evenly—watch constantly because they brown very quickly. Tip the sesame seeds into a small dish and set aside.

3 Once the noodles are tender, add the water chestnuts, bamboo shoots, Napa cabbage, bean sprouts, and scallions to the pan. Return the stock to a boil, stir to mix the ingredients, and let simmer for an additional 2–3 minutes to heat through thoroughly.

4 Carefully drain off 1¼ cups of the stock into a small heatproof pitcher and set aside. Drain and discard any remaining stock and turn the noodles and vegetables into a warmed serving dish. Quickly mix the soy sauce with the reserved stock and pour over the noodles and vegetables. Season to taste with pepper and serve at once.

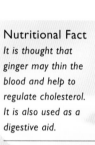

Nutritional Fact

It is thought that ginger may thin the blood and help to regulate cholesterol. It is also used as a digestive aid.

Serving Analysis

- *Calories* 336
- *Protein* 16g
- *Carbohydrate* 58g
- *Sugars* 4.4g
- *Fat* 5.8g
- *Saturates* 1g

Desserts & Baking

Many desserts and cakes are laden with fat and sugar—this is what makes them so tasty and yearned for! This chapter shows how traditional recipes such as crumbles, cheesecakes, and oat bars can be made healthier by reducing the fat and sugar content, but without cutting out the good taste factor. Desserts can also play an important part in helping to achieve the recommended five-a-day portions of fruit and vegetables.

    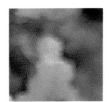 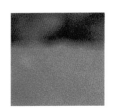

Nutritional Fact
Using unsweetened cocoa rather than melted chocolate gives a good chocolate flavor without the high saturated fat and sugar content found in chocolate.

Serving Analysis
- Calories   232
- Protein   6.4g
- Carbohydrate   42g
- Sugars   29g
- Fat   5.6g
- Saturates   1.9g

serves 4–6

Chocolate Pear Roulade

Ingredients

corn oil, for oiling

scant $^1/_3$ cup all-purpose flour

1 heaping tbsp unsweetened cocoa, plus 1 tsp for dusting

2 eggs

scant $^1/_2$ cup superfine sugar

1 tbsp hot water

1 orange, halved

2 ripe pears

$^7/_8$ cup lowfat mascarpone cheese

1 Preheat the oven to 400°F/200°C. Line a 10$^3/_4$- x 6$^1/_2$-inch/27- x 17-cm jelly roll pan with waxed paper and oil very lightly.

2 Sift the flour and unsweetened cocoa together into a mixing bowl.

3 Put the eggs and sugar into a warmed, heatproof glass mixing bowl and whisk until pale in color and a trail is left when the whisk is lifted out of the mixture. This will take approximately 15 minutes if using an electric hand mixer. (If using a manual hand mixer, the mixture can be whisked over a pan of hot but not boiling water to help reduce the whisking time.)

4 Carefully fold the flour mixture into the whisked egg mixture using a metal tablespoon. Stir in the hot water. Pour the mixture into the prepared pan and gently tilt to level the mixture. Bake in the preheated oven for 8–10 minutes, or until the point of a sharp knife inserted into the center of the sponge comes out clean.

5 Turn the sponge out onto a sheet of waxed paper placed over a clean dish towel. Carefully peel the lining paper off the sponge and trim any crisp edges with a sharp knife.

6 Using the waxed paper under the sponge, loosely roll up the sponge from the short end and let cool completely on a wire rack.

7 Meanwhile, squeeze the juice from 1 orange half into a bowl. Peel, quarter, and core the pears. Thinly slice and toss in the juice to prevent discoloration. Slice the remaining orange half and set aside for decoration.

8 Carefully unroll the cooled sponge and spread with the mascarpone cheese, leaving a 1-inch/2.5-cm border. Drain any excess orange juice from the pears. Set aside a few pear slices for decoration and cover the mascarpone cheese with the remaining slices. Carefully reroll the sponge.

9 Using a sharp knife, slice the roulade into portions and serve on plates decorated with the reserved pear and orange slices. Lightly sift over the unsweetened cocoa and serve at once. This dessert is best eaten on the day it is made—any leftover roulade should be stored in the refrigerator and consumed within 24 hours.

serves 4–6

Peach & Apple Crumble

Ingredients

1 cooking apple
2 eating apples
$^1/_2$ cup cold water
14 oz/400 g canned peach slices in fruit juice, drained
scant $^5/_8$ cup all-purpose flour
$^5/_8$ cup rolled oats
generous $^1/_4$ cup firmly packed raw brown sugar
2 oz/55 g polyunsaturated spread
custard made with skim milk, lowfat plain mascarpone cheese, or yogurt, to serve

Nutritional Fact

Apples contain high levels of pectin, a type of fiber, which is particularly good at carrying toxins out of the body. They also have good levels of potassium to aid heart health.

Serving Analysis

- Calories   315
- Protein   3.4g
- Carbohydrate   54g
- Sugars   32g
- Fat   9.9g
- Saturates   1.8g

1 Preheat the oven to 375°F/190°C. Peel, core, and slice the apples and put into a small pan with the water. Bring to a boil, then cover and let simmer, stirring occasionally, for 4–5 minutes, or until just tender. Remove from the heat and drain away any excess liquid. Stir the drained peach slices into the apple and transfer the fruit to a 4-cup ovenproof dish.

2 Meanwhile, combine the flour, oats, and sugar in a mixing bowl. Rub in the spread with your fingertips until the mixture resembles fine bread crumbs.

3 Sprinkle the crumble topping evenly over the fruit and bake in the preheated oven for 20 minutes, or until golden brown. Serve warm with custard made with skim milk, or lowfat plain mascarpone cheese, or yogurt. This dessert is best eaten on the day it is made—any leftover crumble should be stored in the refrigerator and consumed within 24 hours.

serves 4

Blueberry Fools

Ingredients

1 heaping tbsp custard powder

1 1/4 cups skim or semiskim milk

2 tbsp superfine sugar

scant 3/4 cup fresh or frozen blueberries, thawed if frozen

7/8 cup lowfat mascarpone cheese

1 Blend the custard powder with 1/4 cup of the milk in a heatproof bowl. Bring the remaining milk to a boil in a small pan and pour over the custard mixture, mixing well. Return the custard to the pan and return to a boil over medium–low heat, stirring constantly, until thickened. Pour the custard into the bowl and sprinkle the sugar over the top of the custard to prevent a skin forming. Cover and let cool completely.

2 Set aside 12 blueberries for decoration. Put the remaining blueberries and cold custard into a blender and process until smooth.

3 Spoon the mascarpone cheese and blueberry mixture in alternate layers into 4 tall glasses. Decorate with the reserved blueberries and serve at once.

Nutritional Fact

Blueberries are rich in vitamin C, which is an antioxidant and may boost the immune system. They are also rich in anthocyanins, plant chemicals that help to promote heart health.

Serving Analysis

- *Calories*   *133*
- *Protein*   *5.9g*
- *Carbohydrate*   *22g*
- *Sugars*   *20.6g*
- *Fat*   *2.8g*
- *Saturates*   *1.5g*

serves 4

Exotic Fruit Cocktail

Nutritional Fact

Pineapple contains a substance called bromelain, which has been shown to reduce blood pressure effectively and help prevent heart disease.

Serving Analysis

- Calories   152
- Protein   2g
- Carbohydrate   38g
- Sugars   31.4g
- Fat   0.9g
- Saturates   0.1g

Ingredients

2 oranges

2 large passion fruit

1 pineapple

1 pomegranate

1 banana

1 Cut 1 orange in half and squeeze the juice into a bowl, discarding any pips. Using a sharp knife, cut away all the peel and pith from the second orange. Working over the bowl to catch the juice, carefully cut the orange segments between the membranes to obtain skinless segments of fruit. Discard any pips.

2 Cut the passion fruit in half, scoop the flesh into a nylon strainer and, using a spoon, push the pulp and juice into the bowl of orange segments. Discard the pips.

3 Using a sharp knife, cut away all the skin from the pineapple and cut the flesh lengthwise into quarters. Cut away the central hard core. Cut the flesh into chunks and add to the orange and passion fruit mixture. Cover and let chill the fruit at this stage if you are not serving at once.

4 Cut the pomegranate into quarters and, using your fingers or a teaspoon, remove the red seeds from the membrane. Cover and let chill until ready to serve—do not add too early to the fruit cocktail because the seeds discolor the other fruit.

5 Just before serving, peel and slice the banana, add to the fruit cocktail with the pomegranate seeds, and mix thoroughly. Serve at once.

serves 4

Broiled Cinnamon Oranges

Ingredients

4 large oranges

1 tsp ground cinnamon

1 tbsp raw brown sugar

1 Preheat the broiler to high. Cut the oranges in half and discard any pips. Using a sharp or curved grapefruit knife, carefully cut the flesh away from the skin by cutting around the edge of the fruit. Cut across the segments to loosen the flesh into bite-size pieces that will spoon out easily.

2 Place the orange halves, cut-side up, in a shallow, heatproof dish. Mix the cinnamon with the sugar in a small bowl and sprinkle evenly over the orange halves. Cook under the preheated broiler for 3–5 minutes, or until the sugar has caramelized and is golden and bubbling. Serve at once.

Nutritional Fact

In Asian medicine, cinnamon has long been used to treat high blood pressure and poor blood circulation.

Serving Analysis

- *Calories* 72
- *Protein* 1.2g
- *Carbohydrate* 18g
- *Sugars* 14.7g
- *Fat* 0.2g
- *Saturates* 0.02g

makes 10

Apricot Oat Bars

Ingredients

corn oil, for oiling

6 oz/175 g polyunsaturated spread

scant $^1/_2$ cup raw brown sugar

$^1/_8$ cup honey

scant 1 cup dried apricots, chopped

2 tsp sesame seeds

2$^1/_2$ cups rolled oats

1 Preheat the oven to 350°F/180°C. Very lightly oil a 10$^1/_2$- × 6$^1/_2$-inch/26- × 17-cm shallow baking pan.

2 Put the spread, sugar, and honey into a small pan over low heat and heat until the ingredients have melted together—do not boil. When the ingredients are warm and well combined, stir in the apricots, sesame seeds, and oats.

3 Spoon the mixture into the prepared pan and lightly level with the back of a spoon. Cook in the preheated oven for 20–25 minutes, or until golden brown. Remove from the oven, cut into 10 bars, and let cool completely before removing from the baking pan. Store the oat bars in an airtight container and consume within 2–3 days.

Nutritional Fact
Oats are a fantastic source of slow-releasing energy. Sesame seeds contain omega oils that are important for heart health and cholesterol regulation.

Serving Analysis

- *Calories*   293
- *Protein*   3.6g
- *Carbohydrate*   34g
- *Sugars*   20g
- *Fat*   16.5g
- *Saturates*   2.9g

Makes one 1 lb/450 g loaf—10–12 slices

Golden Raisin Tealoaf

Ingredients

corn oil, for oiling

scant 1/2 cup bran flakes

2/3 cup golden raisins

scant 1/2 cup firmly packed raw brown sugar

1 1/4 cups skim or semiskim milk

scant 1 1/2 cups self-rising flour

tea or freshly squeezed fruit juice, to serve

Nutritional Fact

Just 1 tablespoon of dried fruit counts as one of the five portions of fruit and vegetables recommended per day.

Serving Analysis

• Calories	156
• Protein	3.5g
• Carbohydrate	34g
• Sugars	16.6g
• Fat	1.3g
• Saturates	0.5g

1 Very lightly oil a 1-lb/450-g loaf pan and line the bottom with waxed paper.

2 Put the bran flakes, golden raisins, sugar, and milk into a mixing bowl, cover, and let soak for at least 1 hour in the refrigerator, or until the bran flakes have softened and the fruit has plumped up after absorbing some of the milk—the mixture can be left overnight in the refrigerator.

3 Preheat the oven to 375°F/190°C. Stir the flour into the soaked ingredients, mix well, and spoon into the loaf pan. Bake in the preheated oven for 40–45 minutes, or until the point of a sharp knife inserted into the center of the loaf comes out clean. Let cool in the pan on a wire rack.

4 When cold, turn the loaf out, and discard the lining paper. Serve in slices with cups of tea or glasses of freshly squeezed fruit juice. Store any leftover loaf in an airtight container and consume within 2–3 days.

serves 4

Mango Cheesecakes

1 Line the bottom and sides of 4 x ⅔-cup ramekins with waxed paper and very lightly oil.

2 Melt the spread in a small pan over low heat, remove from the heat, and stir in the ginger and oats. Mix thoroughly and let cool.

3 Using a sharp knife, cut the mango lengthwise down either side of the thin central seed. Peel the flesh. Cut away any flesh from around the seed and peel. Cut the flesh into chunks and set aside 4 oz/115 g. Put the remaining mango flesh into a food processor or blender and process until smooth. Transfer to a small bowl.

4 Drain away any excess fluid from the cheeses and, using a fork or tablespoon, blend together in a bowl. Finely chop the reserved mango flesh and stir into the cheese mixture along with 1 tablespoon of the mango purée. Divide the cheesecake filling evenly between the ramekins and level with the back of a spoon. Cover each cheesecake evenly with the cooled oat mixture and let chill in the refrigerator for at least 3 hours for the filling to firm. Cover and let chill the mango purée.

5 To serve, carefully trim the lining paper level with the oat mixture. Since the oat base is crumbly, place an individual serving plate on top of a ramekin when turning out the cheesecakes. Holding firmly, turn both over to invert. Carefully remove the ramekin and peel away the lining paper. Repeat for the remaining cheesecakes. Spoon the mango purée around each cheesecake and decorate the top of each with 3 raspberries, if using. Serve at once.

Ingredients

corn oil, for oiling

2 tbsp polyunsaturated spread

½ tsp ground ginger

⅝ cup rolled oats

1 large ripe mango, about
1 lb 5 oz/600 g

1⅛ cups virtually fat-free Quark soft cheese

scant ½ cup medium-fat soft cheese

12 raspberries, to decorate (optional)

Nutritional Fact
Mangoes are a good source of fiber, beta-carotene, and vitamin C. They are also thought to help aid digestion and cleanse the blood.

Serving Analysis
* Calories   259
* Protein   14g
* Carbohydrate   23g
* Sugars   11.7g
* Fat   12g
* Saturates   3.8g

Index